Trailblazers in the Making for Student Career Success

Cheryl

Copyright © [2023]

Title: Trailblazers in the Making: Paving the Way for Student Career Success
Author's: Cheryl

This book was printed and published by [Publisher's: **Cheryl**] in [2023]

ISBN:

TABLE OF CONTENT

Chapter 4: Developing a Career Plan   25

Assessing Your Skills and Knowledge Gaps

Identifying Opportunities for Skill Development and Training

Creating a Timeline for Achieving Career Milestones

Chapter 5: Building a Strong Professional Network   31

Understanding the Importance of Networking

Strategies for Building and Expanding Your Network

Leveraging Social Media for Professional Connections

Chapter 6: Enhancing Your Professional Brand   37

Defining Your Personal Brand

Crafting an Effective Resume and Cover Letter

Building an Online Presence through LinkedIn and Personal Websites

Chapter 10: Overcoming Challenges and Obstacles 61

Dealing with Rejections and Setbacks

Managing Work-Life Balance and Burnout

Building Resilience and Adaptability in the Face of Challenges

Chapter 11: Celebrating Career Milestones 67

Recognizing and Appreciating Your Achievements

Setting New Goals and Ambitions

Inspiring Others on Their Career Journeys

Chapter 12: Trailblazers in Action: Inspiring Student Success Stories 73

Sharing Stories of Successful Students and Their Career Paths

Lessons Learned from Trailblazers in Various Fields

Motivating and Empowering Students to Pursue Their Dreams

Chapter 1: The Importance of Career Success

Understanding the Significance of Career Success

Success Changes Your Life

Introduction:

In today's fast-paced world, career success holds immense significance for students. It not only shapes their professional life but also impacts their overall well-being and personal growth. This subchapter explores the profound significance of career success, emphasizing how it can transform lives and open doors to endless possibilities.

1. A Sense of Accomplishment:

Achieving career success brings an unparalleled sense of accomplishment. It validates the hard work, determination, and sacrifices made along the way. As students strive for success, they learn valuable skills such as goal-setting, perseverance, and resilience, which become essential life tools. The feeling of accomplishment boosts self-confidence, empowering students to pursue their dreams fearlessly.

2. Financial Stability:

Career success often translates into financial stability, enabling students to support themselves and their families. Financial independence allows individuals to access better opportunities, invest in personal growth, and contribute to society. It frees them from the constraints of financial worries, promoting a higher quality of life and the ability to pursue passions without financial limitations.

3. Professional Growth and Personal Fulfillment:

Success in one's chosen career path leads to continuous professional growth. It allows students to expand their knowledge, gain experience, and climb the ladder of success. With each achievement, individuals experience personal fulfillment, knowing that they are making a difference in their chosen field. Professional growth also opens doors to exciting opportunities, networking, and the chance to leave a lasting impact.

4. Increased Influence and Recognition:

Career success brings with it increased influence and recognition. As students excel in their chosen fields, their achievements and expertise are acknowledged and celebrated. This recognition not only boosts self-esteem but also elevates their professional profile. Students become role models, inspiring others and creating a positive impact on their communities.

5. Expanding Horizons:

Success in one's career allows for the exploration of new horizons. It provides the freedom to take risks, venture into uncharted territory, and embrace new challenges. Students who achieve career success often find themselves at the forefront of innovation and change, shaping industries and making a significant difference in the world.

Conclusion:

Understanding the significance of career success is crucial for students. It is not only a reflection of their hard work and dedication but also a gateway to a fulfilled and prosperous life. By recognizing the transformative power of career success, students can pave their own paths, overcome obstacles, and become trailblazers in their chosen fields. Embrace the journey, strive for excellence, and unlock the endless possibilities that come with a successful career.

The Impact of Career Success on Personal Growth and Fulfillment

In the journey of life, one of the most significant factors that can shape our overall happiness and fulfillment is our career success. Our professional achievements not only provide financial stability but also have a profound impact on our personal growth and development. This subchapter aims to explore the transformative effects of career success on individuals, highlighting how it can pave the way for a more fulfilling and purposeful life.

Career success opens doors to new opportunities and experiences that can broaden our horizons and expand our knowledge. Achieving professional milestones often requires acquiring new skills, stepping out of our comfort zones, and embracing challenges. Through these experiences, we not only enhance our expertise in a specific field but also cultivate a growth mindset that can be applied to various aspects of our lives. Success in our careers exposes us to new ideas, networks, and perspectives, fostering personal growth and a deeper understanding of the world around us.

Moreover, career success allows us to gain a sense of purpose and direction in life. When we excel in our chosen paths, we feel a profound sense of accomplishment and satisfaction. This fulfillment contributes to our overall well-being and happiness, empowering us to lead a meaningful life. As students, it is crucial to recognize that investing in our education and pursuing our passions can lead to a fulfilling career that aligns with our values and aspirations.

Successful individuals often become role models and trailblazers in their respective fields. Their achievements inspire others to strive for greatness and make a positive impact on society. By achieving career success, students have the opportunity to become influential leaders, change-makers, and advocates for important causes. The impact of their success extends far beyond personal accomplishments, as it can inspire and empower others to follow their dreams and pursue their own paths to success.

However, it is important to note that career success is not solely defined by external achievements or societal recognition. True success lies in finding fulfillment and aligning our professional endeavors with our personal values and passions. It is essential for students to reflect on their own definition of success and ensure that their career choices contribute to their overall growth and happiness.

In conclusion, career success has a profound impact on personal growth and fulfillment. It opens doors to new experiences, enhances our skills, and provides a sense of purpose and direction. As students, we should strive for success in our chosen paths, not only for financial stability but also to lead a fulfilling and meaningful life. By embracing challenges, pursuing our passions, and aligning our professional endeavors with our personal values, we can become trailblazers in our own right, paving the way for a future filled with success and personal growth.

Chapter 2: Exploring Different Career Paths

Identifying Your Interests and Passions

One of the most important steps in paving your way to career success is identifying your interests and passions. When you truly understand what drives you and what you are passionate about, you will be able to make informed decisions about your future and pursue a path that brings you fulfillment and satisfaction. In this subchapter, we will explore various strategies to help you uncover your interests and passions, ultimately setting you on a path towards success that can change your life.

To begin, it is crucial to take the time for self-reflection. Consider what activities or subjects bring you joy and excitement. Reflect on moments when you felt a sense of accomplishment or when time seemed to fly by because you were so immersed in what you were doing. These experiences can provide valuable insights into your passions and interests.

Another effective way to identify your interests is by exploring a wide range of experiences. Take advantage of opportunities to try new things, whether it be joining clubs, attending workshops, or volunteering in different fields. By exposing yourself to various activities, you will be able to gauge your level of interest and see what resonates with you the most.

Additionally, seeking guidance from mentors and professionals can be immensely beneficial. Reach out to individuals who are already successful in fields that intrigue you. They can provide valuable advice and share their own experiences, helping you gain clarity about your own passions. Networking events, career fairs, and informational interviews are great platforms to connect with these individuals.

Moreover, it is essential to consider your strengths and talents. Reflect on the skills and abilities that come naturally to you. Identifying your strengths can provide valuable guidance in choosing a career path that aligns with your abilities and allows you to excel.

Lastly, don't be afraid to think outside the box and challenge societal expectations. Your interests and passions may not fit into traditional career paths, and that is perfectly fine. Pursuing a unique and unconventional path can lead to extraordinary opportunities and ultimately change your life for the better.

In conclusion, identifying your interests and passions is a crucial step in paving the way for your career success. By engaging in self-reflection, exploring new experiences, seeking guidance, considering your strengths, and thinking outside the box, you can uncover what truly drives you. Remember, success changes your life, and by pursuing a career that aligns with your passions, you can achieve not only professional success but also personal fulfillment and happiness.

Researching Various Career Options

As students, you are at a crucial stage in your life where the decisions you make today can shape your future. Choosing a career path is one such decision that will significantly impact your life. It is essential to explore various career options before making a choice, as success in your chosen field can truly transform your life.

Researching different career options provides you with valuable insights into the opportunities available and helps you make an informed decision. Here are some steps you can take to embark on your career exploration journey:

1. Self-Reflection: Begin by reflecting on your interests, skills, values, and passions. What subjects do you enjoy the most? What activities make you feel fulfilled? Understanding yourself better will help you identify potential career paths that align with your strengths and personal values.

2. Online Resources: Utilize the vast array of online resources available to research different careers. Visit career websites, read industry blogs, and explore job descriptions to gain a deeper understanding of the roles and responsibilities associated with various professions.

3. Networking: Reach out to professionals already working in fields that interest you. Attend career fairs, join professional organizations, and engage in informational interviews. Networking allows you to learn from individuals with firsthand experience and gain valuable insights into the realities of different careers.

4. Internships and Job Shadowing: Consider participating in internships or job shadowing opportunities to gain practical experience in different industries. These experiences provide a glimpse into what a typical workday looks like and can help you determine if a particular career is the right fit for you.

5. Guidance Counselors and Mentors: Seek guidance from your school's counselors or mentors who can provide personalized advice based on your individual goals and aspirations. They can help you navigate the vast sea of career options and assist you in finding resources to further explore your interests.

Remember, success changes your life. By researching various career options, you are taking a proactive step towards creating a fulfilling future. Take the time to explore different paths, consider your passions and skills, and seek guidance from those who can support you along the way. With thorough research and self-reflection, you will find a career that aligns with your goals and passions, paving the way for a successful and meaningful life.

Gaining Insights from Professionals in Different Fields

Success Changes Your Life

In today's rapidly changing world, students are faced with the challenge of making important decisions about their future careers. The choices they make now will have a significant impact on their lives for years to come. As students, it is crucial to gain insights from professionals in different fields who have already paved the way to success. By learning from their experiences, students can make informed decisions and set themselves on the path to achieving their goals.

The subchapter "Gaining Insights from Professionals in Different Fields" aims to provide students with valuable advice and perspectives from successful individuals who have achieved remarkable accomplishments in their respective fields. These trailblazers have faced numerous challenges, overcame obstacles, and ultimately emerged as successful professionals. By sharing their stories, they can inspire and guide students towards their own career success.

The subchapter delves into various professions, ranging from business and entrepreneurship to science, arts, and technology. Students will have the opportunity to explore the journeys of renowned individuals who have made significant contributions in these fields. Through interviews and personal anecdotes, these professionals will share their insights, strategies, and lessons learned along the way.

Students will learn about the importance of perseverance, resilience, and continuous learning. They will discover how successful individuals have overcome setbacks and used them as stepping stones to reach higher levels of achievement. The subchapter will also highlight the significance of networking, mentorship, and seizing opportunities in the pursuit of career success.

Moreover, the subchapter will emphasize the importance of aligning one's passion and interests with their chosen career path. Students will understand the value of pursuing a profession that resonates with their talents and values, as this is vital for long-term fulfillment and personal growth.

By gaining insights from professionals in different fields, students will be empowered to make informed decisions about their own career paths. They will understand that success is not always linear but rather a lifelong journey of growth and self-discovery. This subchapter will serve as a roadmap for students, paving the way for their own trailblazing careers and paving the way for a successful and fulfilling life.

Chapter 3: Setting Career Goals

The Value of Setting Clear and Measurable Goals

Success Changes Your Life

Introduction:

In today's competitive world, success is not just a destination; it's a way of life. As students, you have embarked on a journey that will shape your future and determine the path you take. To pave the way for your career success, it is crucial to understand the value of setting clear and measurable goals. This subchapter will delve into why goal-setting is essential and how it can transform your life.

The Power of Goal-Setting:

Setting clear and measurable goals provides a roadmap for success. Without a target in sight, you may wander aimlessly and struggle to make progress. Goals provide direction, focus, and motivation, enabling you to make purposeful decisions and take decisive actions. By defining your goals, you become proactive in designing your future, rather than merely reacting to circumstances.

Clarity Breeds Success:

Clear goals act as a compass, guiding you towards your desired outcomes. When you have a crystal-clear vision of what you want to achieve, it becomes easier to stay committed, overcome obstacles, and make the necessary sacrifices. Clarity allows you to prioritize your actions, eliminating distractions and ensuring that every step you take is aligned with your ultimate objectives.

Measuring Progress:

Measurable goals enable you to track your progress and evaluate your performance. By breaking down your larger goals into smaller, achievable milestones, you create a sense of accomplishment and momentum. Regularly monitoring your progress allows you to identify areas for improvement, make necessary adjustments, and celebrate your successes along the way.

Boosting Motivation:

Setting goals provides a sense of purpose and fuels your inner motivation. When you have a clear target to strive for, you become more focused and driven. Goals create a sense of urgency, pushing you to step out of your comfort zone and embrace challenges. With each milestone achieved, your confidence and enthusiasm grow, propelling you forward towards even greater achievements.

Conclusion:

In the journey of paving the way for your career success, setting clear and measurable goals is an invaluable tool. Goals provide direction, clarity, and motivation, allowing you to navigate the challenges and uncertainties with confidence. By defining your goals, measuring your progress, and staying committed, you can transform your life and become a trailblazer in your chosen field. Remember, success is not a destination, but a lifelong journey, and it all starts with setting clear and measurable goals.

Creating a Vision for Your Ideal Career

In our journey towards a successful and fulfilling career, one of the most crucial steps is to create a vision for our ideal future. Visualizing our dream career not only helps us gain clarity and direction, but also serves as a powerful motivation to turn our aspirations into reality. This subchapter will guide students on how to create a vision for their ideal career and pave the way for their own success.

To begin, it is important to understand that success has the power to change your life in countless ways. It goes beyond financial stability and encompasses personal growth, happiness, and fulfillment. By envisioning your ideal career, you are setting yourself up for a life that aligns with your passions, values, and strengths.

Start by self-reflecting on what truly makes you happy and what you are passionate about. What activities or subjects excite you? What are your natural talents and skills? Consider these questions as you envision your ideal career. It's essential to choose a path that resonates with your authentic self, as this will fuel your drive and determination to achieve your goals.

Next, think about the impact you want to make in the world through your work. How do you want to contribute to society? What problems or challenges do you want to solve? By aligning your vision with a higher purpose, you will find greater meaning and fulfillment in your career.

Once you have a clearer picture of your ideal career, set specific goals and create a plan to achieve them. Break down your long-term vision into smaller, achievable steps. Identify the skills, knowledge, and experiences you need to acquire along the way. Seek mentorship and guidance from professionals in your field of interest to gain valuable insights and advice.

Finally, embrace a growth mindset and remain adaptable to change. The path to success is rarely linear, and setbacks and obstacles are inevitable. Stay open to new opportunities and be willing to adjust your vision as you grow and evolve. Remember, success is a journey, and your ideal career will continue to evolve as you gain new experiences and insights.

In conclusion, creating a vision for your ideal career is an essential step towards paving the way for your own success. By envisioning a future that aligns with your passions, values, and purpose, you can chart a course that leads to personal growth, happiness, and fulfillment. Stay committed to your vision, set goals, and embrace a growth mindset as you navigate your path to success. Your dream career is within reach, and by following this guidance, you can become a trailblazer in your own right.

Setting Short-term and Long-term Career Goals

In today's fast-paced and competitive world, it is crucial for students to have a clear vision of their career goals. Whether you are in high school, college, or just starting your professional journey, setting short-term and long-term career goals can pave the way for your success and transform your life.

Short-term goals are the stepping stones that lead to long-term success. These goals are typically achievable within a year or less and help you focus on immediate actions. For instance, if you aspire to become a software engineer, your short-term goals might include completing coding courses, participating in internships, or networking with professionals in the field. By setting and accomplishing short-term goals, you gain valuable experience and skills that contribute to your long-term career objectives.

On the other hand, long-term career goals provide a broader perspective and guide your overall direction. These goals generally extend beyond five years and are instrumental in shaping your desired career path. For example, if you dream of becoming a renowned doctor, your long-term goals may involve pursuing a medical degree, specializing in a specific field, and establishing your own practice. By setting long-term goals, you gain a sense of purpose, motivation, and clarity about the steps you need to take to achieve your ultimate career aspirations.

To effectively set short-term and long-term career goals, it is essential to follow a structured approach. Start by reflecting on your passions, interests, and values. What are you truly passionate about? What drives you? Identifying your core values and aligning them with your career goals will ensure that you embark on a path that brings you fulfillment and satisfaction.

Next, break down your long-term goals into smaller, manageable short-term goals. This breakdown helps you create a roadmap with measurable milestones that you can track your progress against. Remember to set realistic and achievable goals, as this will boost your confidence and keep you motivated throughout your journey.

Additionally, seek guidance from mentors, career counselors, or professionals in your desired field. They can offer valuable insights, advice, and support to help you refine your goals and make informed decisions. Networking with individuals who have already achieved success in your niche can open doors to opportunities and provide valuable connections.

In conclusion, setting short-term and long-term career goals is vital for student success. By mapping out your desired career path and breaking it down into achievable milestones, you can navigate the challenges and uncertainties of the future with confidence. Remember, success changes your life, and by setting goals, you are taking the first step towards transforming your dreams into reality.

Chapter 4: Developing a Career Plan

Assessing Your Skills and Knowledge Gaps

In the journey towards success, it is crucial for students to assess their skills and knowledge gaps. Identifying these areas of improvement is the first step towards paving the way for a successful career. This subchapter, "Assessing Your Skills and Knowledge Gaps," aims to guide students in understanding the importance of self-assessment and providing practical strategies for identifying and bridging these gaps.

Self-assessment is an essential tool that allows students to gain insight into their strengths and weaknesses. By reflecting on their skills and knowledge, students can pinpoint areas that require improvement. It is important to approach this process with an open mind and a willingness to embrace growth. By acknowledging where improvements are needed, students can take proactive steps towards enhancing their abilities and increasing their chances of success.

One effective strategy for assessing skills and knowledge gaps is self-reflection. Students can create a list of their strengths and weaknesses, focusing on areas that are directly related to their desired career path. This exercise helps students gain clarity on their skill set and identify areas that need development. Additionally, seeking feedback from mentors, teachers, or professionals in the field can provide valuable insights and further highlight areas for improvement.

Another valuable tool for self-assessment is conducting research on industry trends and requirements. By staying up-to-date with the latest advancements and demands within their chosen field, students can identify gaps in their knowledge. This research can be done through reading industry publications, attending workshops or seminars, or connecting with professionals in the field. This not only helps students identify their knowledge gaps but also showcases their commitment to continuous learning.

Once students have identified their skills and knowledge gaps, it is crucial to develop a plan to bridge these gaps. This can involve enrolling in relevant courses, participating in internships or apprenticeships, or seeking out additional learning opportunities. By actively seeking out experiences that enhance their skill set, students can demonstrate their dedication to personal growth and increase their chances of success.

In conclusion, assessing skills and knowledge gaps is a vital step towards student career success. By acknowledging areas that need improvement, students can take proactive steps to enhance their abilities and increase their chances of achieving their goals. Self-reflection, seeking feedback, and conducting research on industry trends are effective strategies for identifying these gaps. By developing a plan to bridge these gaps, students can pave the way for a successful and fulfilling career. Remember, success changes your life, so take charge of your journey by assessing and addressing your skills and knowledge gaps.

Identifying Opportunities for Skill Development and Training

In today's rapidly evolving world, success changes lives, and one of the key drivers of success is skill development and training. As students, you have the incredible opportunity to pave the way for your own career success. This subchapter, "Identifying Opportunities for Skill Development and Training," aims to guide you through the process of identifying and seizing these opportunities.

Skill development is a continuous process that involves acquiring and honing abilities that are relevant to your chosen field or desired career path. By investing time and effort into developing your skills, you will not only enhance your employability but also expand your horizons and unlock countless opportunities.

To begin your journey towards skill development, it is essential to identify the areas where you can grow and excel. Start by reflecting on your strengths and weaknesses. What are you naturally good at, and which skills do you need to improve upon? Consider your interests and passions as well. Aligning your skill development with your passions will not only make the process more enjoyable but also increase your motivation to excel.

Once you have identified your areas of focus, it's time to explore the various training opportunities available to you. Traditional education, such as attending college or university, is undoubtedly valuable. However, it is essential to recognize that learning doesn't stop at graduation. Seek out additional training programs, workshops, and certifications that can enhance your skill set. Online platforms, such as Coursera, Udemy, and LinkedIn Learning, offer a wide range of courses covering various subjects, including business, technology, marketing, and more.

Another crucial aspect of skill development is gaining practical experience. Look for internships, part-time jobs, or volunteer opportunities that align with your career interests. Practical experience not only allows you to apply the skills you have learned but also helps you build a network and gain valuable insights into your chosen field.

It's worth mentioning that skill development is not limited to technical abilities alone. Soft skills, including communication, teamwork, problem-solving, and leadership, are equally important in today's job market. Seek opportunities to develop these skills through extracurricular activities, group projects, or by taking on leadership roles in student organizations.

Remember, success changes lives, and skill development is the key to unlocking that success. By identifying the areas where you can grow, exploring training opportunities, gaining practical experience, and developing both technical and soft skills, you will position yourself as a trailblazer in your chosen field. Embrace the journey of skill development, for it is the path that leads to a fulfilling and successful career.

Creating a Timeline for Achieving Career Milestones

In today's fast-paced world, success can truly change your life. As students, you hold the key to unlocking your potential and achieving your career goals. However, the path to success is rarely a straight line. It requires careful planning, dedication, and a well-thought-out timeline. In this subchapter, we will explore the importance of creating a timeline for achieving career milestones and how it can pave the way for your student career success.

A timeline is like a roadmap that helps you navigate through the various stages of your career journey. It allows you to set clear goals, map out the steps needed to achieve them, and stay organized along the way. By creating a timeline, you can break down your long-term goals into smaller, manageable tasks, making it easier to stay focused and motivated.

The first step in creating a timeline is to identify your career milestones. These milestones can be anything from completing an internship, gaining specific skills, or securing a job in your desired field. Take some time to reflect on your long-term goals and determine the key milestones that will lead you there.

Once you have identified your milestones, it's time to set deadlines. Deadlines provide a sense of urgency and help you prioritize your tasks. Be realistic with your deadlines, considering the time and resources required to achieve each milestone. Remember that timelines can be adjusted as needed, so don't be afraid to modify them along the way.

Next, break down each milestone into smaller, actionable steps. For example, if one of your milestones is gaining a specific skill, your steps may include researching training programs, enrolling in courses, practicing, and seeking opportunities to apply your newly acquired skills. Assign deadlines to each step to ensure progress is made consistently.

To stay organized and track your progress, consider using a calendar or a project management tool. These tools can help you visualize your timeline, set reminders, and monitor your achievements. Regularly review your timeline and make adjustments as necessary to stay on track.

Creating a timeline for achieving career milestones is a powerful tool that can propel you towards success. It provides structure, keeps you focused, and ensures that you are making progress towards your goals. Remember, success changes your life, and the journey starts with a well-planned timeline. So, take the time to create your roadmap to success and pave the way for your student career success.

Chapter 5: Building a Strong Professional Network

Understanding the Importance of Networking

In today's fast-paced and ever-evolving world, success goes hand in hand with networking. Whether you are a high school student exploring future career paths or a college student preparing to enter the workforce, understanding the importance of networking is crucial. Networking not only opens doors to new opportunities but also plays a significant role in shaping your future success.

Networking is all about building connections and relationships with people who can offer guidance, support, and opportunities. These connections can be with professionals in your desired field, mentors, alumni, or even fellow students. By engaging in meaningful conversations and building a strong network, you gain access to a wealth of knowledge, experiences, and potential job opportunities.

One of the key benefits of networking is the chance to learn from others who have already achieved success in their respective fields. These trailblazers can provide valuable insights, advice, and guidance, helping you navigate the often challenging path to success. By leveraging their expertise, you can avoid common pitfalls and make informed decisions about your own career journey.

Networking also provides a platform for personal growth and development. Through networking events, workshops, and conferences, you can expand your knowledge, enhance your communication skills, and broaden your horizons. These experiences not only boost your confidence but also allow you to showcase your talents and unique abilities to potential employers and collaborators.

Moreover, networking allows you to tap into the hidden job market. Many job opportunities are never advertised publicly and are instead filled through personal connections. By building a strong network, you increase your chances of being referred to these hidden job openings, giving you a competitive advantage over other candidates.

Additionally, networking provides a supportive community that can offer encouragement, motivation, and a sense of belonging. Surrounding yourself with like-minded individuals who share similar goals and aspirations can push you to strive for excellence and reach your full potential. These connections can also serve as a support system during challenging times, offering guidance and assistance when needed.

In conclusion, networking is a vital component of achieving success and paving the way for a fulfilling career. By actively engaging in networking opportunities, you gain access to a wealth of knowledge, support, and potential job opportunities. Networking not only opens doors to new possibilities but also provides a platform for personal growth and development. So, take every chance to connect with professionals, mentors, and fellow students, as they can play a pivotal role in shaping your future success.

Strategies for Building and Expanding Your Network

In today's competitive job market, building and expanding your network is crucial for success. Your network can open doors to new opportunities, provide valuable insights, and offer support and guidance as you navigate your career path. In this subchapter, we will explore effective strategies for students to build and expand their networks, paving the way for their future success.

1. Start within your circle: Begin by reaching out to friends, classmates, and professors. Attend student organization events, career fairs, and alumni gatherings. These connections can provide a solid foundation for your network and can introduce you to potential mentors or future employers.

2. Leverage social media: Utilize professional networking platforms like LinkedIn to connect with professionals in your field of interest. Join relevant groups and participate in discussions to showcase your knowledge and interests. Engage with industry influencers by commenting on their posts and sharing valuable content.

3. Informational interviews: Reach out to professionals in your desired field and request informational interviews. This is an opportunity to learn more about their career journey, seek advice, and build a connection. Be prepared with thoughtful questions and show genuine interest in their experiences.

4. Attend industry events: Look for conferences, workshops, and seminars in your field. These events provide a platform to meet industry experts, gain insights into current trends, and establish valuable connections. Be proactive in networking by introducing

yourself, exchanging business cards, and following up with a thank-you note.

5. Volunteer and intern: Engaging in volunteer work or internships allows you to meet professionals in your desired industry. It not only provides hands-on experience but also expands your network. Take the initiative to introduce yourself to colleagues, supervisors, and other professionals you encounter during your placement.

6. Give before you receive: Building a network is a two-way street. Offer your support, advice, or resources to others when you can. By providing value to others in your network, you create a mutually beneficial relationship that can lead to future collaborations or recommendations.

7. Maintain and nurture relationships: Building a network is not a one-time task; it requires consistent effort. Stay in touch with your contacts, congratulate them on their achievements, and offer your assistance when needed. Utilize tools like email or social media to stay connected, and make it a habit to reach out periodically.

By implementing these strategies, students can build and expand their networks, setting themselves up for success in their future careers. Remember, success changes your life, and having a strong network can be the key to unlocking new opportunities and achieving your goals. So, start building your network today and pave the way for a successful future.

Leveraging Social Media for Professional Connections

In today's digital age, social media has become an integral part of our lives. It has transformed the way we communicate, connect, and even network professionally. As students on the path to success, it is crucial to understand the power of social media in building and nurturing professional connections that can shape your career trajectory.

Social media platforms such as LinkedIn, Twitter, and even Instagram can serve as powerful tools in expanding your professional network. Gone are the days when networking was limited to attending conferences or industry events. With just a few clicks, you can now connect with professionals from diverse industries and geographical locations, opening up a world of opportunities.

First and foremost, it is essential to create a strong and professional online presence. Your social media profiles should highlight your skills, experiences, and aspirations. Use your bio sections to showcase your unique qualities and interests that set you apart from others. Post relevant content that reflects your professional interests and engage with others in meaningful conversations. By consistently sharing valuable insights and perspectives, you can position yourself as a thought leader in your chosen field.

Furthermore, actively participate in online communities and groups related to your area of interest. Joining professional groups on platforms like LinkedIn allows you to connect with like-minded individuals, exchange ideas, and learn from industry experts. Engaging in discussions and sharing your thoughts will not only help you gain visibility, but it can also lead to valuable connections with professionals who can guide you on your career path.

Remember that social media is a two-way street. It is not just about promoting yourself, but also about supporting and uplifting others. Take the time to acknowledge and appreciate the accomplishments of your connections. Congratulate them on their achievements, share their content, and offer assistance when needed. Building genuine relationships based on mutual support and respect is key to leveraging social media for professional success.

Lastly, always maintain professionalism and be mindful of your online presence. Potential employers and industry leaders often search for candidates online before making hiring decisions. Ensure that your social media profiles are free from inappropriate content and showcase your best self. Use privacy settings effectively to control who can see your posts and always think twice before posting anything that may jeopardize your professional reputation.

Leveraging social media for professional connections can be a game-changer in your journey to success. By harnessing the power of these platforms effectively, you can connect with industry leaders, find mentors, and discover exciting career opportunities that can change your life. Embrace the digital world, build meaningful connections, and pave your way to a successful future.

Chapter 6: Enhancing Your Professional Brand

Defining Your Personal Brand

In today's competitive world, success is not just about academic achievements or professional accomplishments; it's about creating a unique personal brand that sets you apart from the crowd. Your personal brand is a representation of who you are, what you stand for, and what you bring to the table. It is a combination of your skills, values, passions, and experiences that make you memorable and desirable to others.

As students, it's never too early to start thinking about your personal brand. Your journey towards success begins with understanding yourself and what makes you unique. Take the time to reflect on your strengths, weaknesses, and goals. What are your passions? What are the values that drive you? What sets you apart from your peers? These answers will serve as the foundation for building your personal brand.

One key aspect of personal branding is creating a consistent and authentic online presence. In today's digital age, your online presence is often the first impression others have of you. Make sure your social media profiles, such as LinkedIn, Facebook, and Twitter, align with your personal brand. Share content that reflects your interests and expertise, engage with others in your field, and present yourself professionally. Remember, your online presence can help open doors to opportunities and connect you with influential individuals in your industry.

Another important element of personal branding is networking. Success is not achieved in isolation; it requires building relationships with others. Attend industry conferences, join professional organizations, and participate in networking events. Networking allows you to meet like-minded individuals, learn from their experiences, and potentially find mentors who can guide you on your career path. Remember to always be genuine and approachable, as these qualities can leave a lasting impression on others.

Furthermore, personal branding is about showcasing your unique skills and expertise. Develop a portfolio that highlights your achievements, projects, and experiences. This could include academic work, internships, volunteer activities, or any other relevant experiences that demonstrate your abilities. Your portfolio will serve as a tangible representation of your personal brand, allowing others to see the value you bring to the table.

In conclusion, defining your personal brand is crucial for student success. By understanding yourself, creating a consistent online presence, networking, and showcasing your skills, you can pave the way for a successful career. Remember, success changes your life, and by defining your personal brand, you can differentiate yourself in a competitive world and open doors to endless opportunities.

Crafting an Effective Resume and Cover Letter

In today's competitive job market, having a well-crafted resume and cover letter is crucial for achieving career success. Your resume and cover letter are the first impression you make on potential employers, and they can greatly impact your chances of landing an interview. In this subchapter, we will guide you through the process of creating an effective resume and cover letter that will set you apart from other candidates.

The resume is your opportunity to showcase your skills, experiences, and qualifications. It should be concise, well-organized, and tailored to the specific job you are applying for. Start by including your contact information, a professional summary, and a list of your relevant skills. Be sure to highlight any achievements or accomplishments that demonstrate your abilities.

When listing your work experience, focus on the responsibilities and achievements that are most relevant to the job you are applying for. Use action verbs and quantify your accomplishments whenever possible. Additionally, include any relevant internships, volunteer work, or extracurricular activities that demonstrate your skills and commitment.

Your cover letter is an opportunity to expand on the information in your resume and personalize your application. Use it to explain why you are interested in the position and how your skills and experiences make you a strong candidate. Research the company and mention specific details about their mission or values that align with your own.

In both your resume and cover letter, it is important to use professional language and proper formatting. Proofread carefully for any spelling or grammatical errors. Tailor each application to the specific job you are applying for, and avoid using generic templates.

Remember, success changes your life. A well-crafted resume and cover letter can open doors to new opportunities, whether it's an internship, a part-time job, or your dream career. Take the time to carefully craft your application materials, and don't be afraid to seek feedback from mentors or career advisors.

Throughout this subchapter, we will provide you with tips, examples, and resources to help you create a standout resume and cover letter. By investing time and effort into this process, you will increase your chances of success and pave the way for a fulfilling and rewarding career.

Building an Online Presence through LinkedIn and Personal Websites

In today's digital age, having a strong online presence is crucial for success in any career. One platform that has gained immense popularity among professionals is LinkedIn. LinkedIn is not just a platform to connect with colleagues or search for job opportunities; it is a powerful tool that can help you build a strong personal brand and establish your professional identity.

Creating a LinkedIn profile allows you to showcase your skills, education, and work experience in a professional manner. It acts as a virtual resume and provides a platform for potential employers and recruiters to find and learn more about you. By regularly updating your profile with new accomplishments, skills, and projects, you can demonstrate your growth and dedication to your chosen field.

LinkedIn also offers numerous networking opportunities. Joining relevant industry groups and actively participating in discussions can help you connect with like-minded professionals and expand your network. Engaging with others by sharing insightful articles, commenting on posts, and endorsing skills can further enhance your visibility and credibility.

Apart from LinkedIn, having a personal website can significantly boost your online presence. A personal website acts as your online portfolio, allowing you to showcase your work, projects, and achievements in a visually appealing and organized manner. It gives you the freedom to express your creativity and personality, making you stand out from the competition.

Maintaining an active blog on your personal website can also demonstrate your expertise and passion for your chosen field. By regularly publishing insightful articles or sharing your thoughts on industry trends, you can establish yourself as a thought leader and attract the attention of potential employers or clients.

In addition to showcasing your professional accomplishments, a personal website can also provide a platform to highlight your extracurricular activities, volunteer work, or personal interests. This holistic view of your life can help employers or clients understand your values and how you can contribute beyond your professional skills.

It is important to remember that building an online presence takes time and effort. Consistency is key, whether it is regularly updating your LinkedIn profile or maintaining an active blog. By investing in your online presence, you are investing in your future success. A strong online presence can open doors to new opportunities, expand your network, and position you as a trailblazer in your field.

In conclusion, LinkedIn and personal websites are powerful tools for building an online presence and establishing your professional identity. They provide platforms to showcase your skills, connect with industry professionals, and demonstrate your expertise. By leveraging these platforms effectively, you can pave the way for student career success and change your life for the better.

Chapter 7: Mastering Job Interviews

Preparing for Different Types of Interviews

Interviews are a crucial step towards securing your dream job or internship. They provide an opportunity for potential employers to get to know you better and assess your suitability for the role. However, different types of interviews require different approaches and preparations. In this subchapter, we will explore the various types of interviews you may encounter and provide tips on how to prepare for each.

1. Traditional Interviews: These are the most common types of interviews, where you meet face-to-face with the interviewer. To prepare for a traditional interview, research the company thoroughly, understand the job requirements, and practice answering common interview questions. Dress professionally, maintain good eye contact, and exude confidence during the interview.

2. Behavioral Interviews: In this type of interview, employers assess your past experiences and how you handled specific situations. To prepare, think of examples that highlight your skills and achievements. Use the STAR method (Situation, Task, Action, Result) to structure your answers, demonstrating your ability to handle challenges effectively.

3. Panel Interviews: Panel interviews involve multiple interviewers who evaluate your suitability for the job. Research the panel members beforehand to understand their roles and interests. During the

interview, maintain eye contact with all panel members, address each person individually, and be concise in your responses.

4. Phone or Video Interviews: In today's digital age, remote interviews are becoming increasingly popular. Prepare for phone or video interviews by ensuring a stable internet connection, testing your audio and video equipment, and finding a quiet and well-lit space. Dress professionally, maintain good posture, and speak clearly.

5. Case Interviews: Commonly used in consulting and finance industries, case interviews assess your problem-solving skills. Practice solving case studies by breaking down complex problems, identifying key issues, and providing logical solutions. Focus on your thought process and communicate effectively with the interviewer.

Remember, success changes your life, and being well-prepared for different types of interviews can significantly improve your chances of securing your desired role. Practice mock interviews with friends or career advisors, ask for feedback, and continuously refine your interviewing skills. Develop a confident and professional demeanor, highlighting your unique qualities and experiences. By preparing for different types of interviews, you will be well-equipped to impress potential employers and pave the way for your future career success.

Researching the Company and Position

In today's competitive job market, it is crucial for students to go the extra mile when preparing for their future careers. One of the most important steps in this process is researching the company and position you are applying for. By doing thorough research, you can gain valuable insights that will not only impress employers but also help you make informed decisions about your career path.

When researching a company, start by visiting their website. Take the time to explore different sections, such as the "About Us" page, mission and values, and any recent news or press releases. This will give you a good understanding of the company's history, culture, and overall objectives. Additionally, pay attention to their products or services, target audience, and competitive advantages. Knowing these details will enable you to tailor your application and interview responses to align with the company's goals and values.

Furthermore, try to gather information from reliable sources outside of the company's website. Look for news articles, industry reports, and social media accounts that discuss the company or its key players. This will help you get a broader perspective and stay up-to-date with any recent developments or trends in the industry. Employers appreciate candidates who demonstrate a genuine interest in their organization and show that they have done their homework.

While researching the company is essential, it is equally important to delve into the specifics of the position you are applying for. Read the job description carefully and identify the key responsibilities and qualifications required. This will help you understand what the employer is looking for and allow you to highlight relevant skills and experiences in your application materials.

Moreover, try to connect with current or former employees of the company through professional networking platforms like LinkedIn. Reach out to them and politely ask if they would be willing to share their experiences or insights about the company and the position. This firsthand information can provide valuable insights and give you an edge over other candidates.

Ultimately, researching the company and position is a vital step in your career preparation. It allows you to make informed decisions, tailor your application materials, and demonstrate your genuine interest in the organization. By investing time in this process, you are setting yourself up for success and paving the way for a rewarding and fulfilling career. Remember, success changes your life, and thorough research is the first step towards achieving it.

Practicing Interview Questions and Techniques

In today's fast-paced and competitive job market, it is crucial for students to be well-prepared for interviews. Whether you are seeking an internship, part-time job, or your dream career, interview skills play a significant role in determining your success. This subchapter, "Practicing Interview Questions and Techniques," is designed to equip you with the necessary tools to excel in interviews and pave the way for your future success.

The importance of interview preparation cannot be overstated. It is the key to making a positive first impression and distinguishing yourself from other candidates. By practicing interview questions and techniques, you can gain confidence, improve your communication skills, and showcase your unique qualities and strengths.

To begin with, it is essential to research the company or organization you are applying to. Familiarize yourself with their mission, values, and recent accomplishments. This knowledge will not only help you answer questions but also demonstrate your genuine interest and enthusiasm during the interview.

Next, you should anticipate and practice common interview questions. This includes questions about your strengths, weaknesses, past experiences, and your ability to handle challenging situations. By rehearsing your responses, you can ensure that you convey your skills and qualifications effectively.

Additionally, practicing behavioral interview questions can be immensely beneficial. These questions require you to provide examples from your past experiences to showcase your problem-solving abilities, teamwork skills, and leadership qualities. By preparing stories that highlight your achievements and growth, you can leave a lasting impression on the interviewer.

Apart from answering questions, it is crucial to master non-verbal communication techniques. Pay attention to your posture, maintain eye contact, and exhibit confidence through your body language. Practice with a friend or family member and ask for constructive feedback to improve your non-verbal cues.

Lastly, practice mock interviews to simulate a real interview scenario. This will help you manage your nerves, become more comfortable with the interview process, and refine your answers. Record or take notes on your performance, allowing you to identify areas for improvement.

Remember, success changes your life, and excelling in interviews can be the gateway to your dream career. By investing time and effort into practicing interview questions and techniques, you are paving the way for your future success. With preparation and confidence, you can stand out from the competition and seize every opportunity that comes your way. Good luck!

Chapter 8: Excelling in the Workplace

Navigating Organizational Culture and Dynamics

In today's competitive job market, understanding and navigating organizational culture and dynamics is essential for student career success. Organizations are like ecosystems, with their own unique set of values, beliefs, and behaviors that shape the working environment. By recognizing and adapting to these cultural nuances, students can increase their chances of excelling in their careers and making a lasting impact.

Organizational culture refers to the shared values, beliefs, and norms that shape the behavior of individuals within a company. It sets the tone for how employees interact, make decisions, and approach their work. Understanding the culture of an organization is crucial for students as it determines whether they will fit in with the company's ethos and thrive within its environment. Researching and learning about an organization's culture before applying for a job or internship can help students determine if it aligns with their own values and goals.

Navigating organizational dynamics involves understanding the relationships, power structures, and communication patterns within an organization. Students must recognize that every company has its own unique set of dynamics, and being able to adapt and navigate these dynamics is key to success. Building strong relationships with colleagues, supervisors, and mentors is vital for career progression. Students should actively seek out opportunities to network, collaborate, and learn from those who have already achieved success in their chosen field.

Successful individuals understand that organizational culture and dynamics are continuously evolving. As students transition from academia to the professional world, they must be open to learning and adapting to new environments. This flexibility will enable them to thrive in different organizational cultures and effectively navigate the ever-changing dynamics within the workplace. Embracing diversity and inclusion, being curious, and continuously seeking growth opportunities are all strategies that can help students succeed in a variety of organizational contexts.

In conclusion, navigating organizational culture and dynamics is a critical skill for student career success. By understanding and adapting to the unique values, beliefs, and behaviors of different organizations, students can increase their chances of fitting in, excelling, and making a lasting impact. Cultivating strong relationships, being open to learning and growth, and embracing diversity are all strategies that can help students navigate the complexities of the professional world and achieve their career goals. Remember, success changes your life, and being prepared to navigate organizational culture and dynamics will pave the way for a successful and fulfilling career journey.

Building Effective Relationships with Colleagues and Superiors

In the competitive world of today, success is not just about individual accomplishments, but also about building effective relationships with colleagues and superiors. In this subchapter, we will explore the essential skills and strategies that students need to cultivate in order to foster positive relationships in the workplace, paving the way for their own career success.

First and foremost, it is crucial to understand that effective relationships are built on trust and mutual respect. As students embark on their professional journeys, they should strive to be reliable, honest, and accountable. By consistently delivering on promises and demonstrating integrity, students can earn the trust and respect of their colleagues and superiors.

Furthermore, communication plays a vital role in building effective relationships. Students should learn to listen actively, seeking to understand the perspectives and ideas of others. By actively engaging in conversations and demonstrating empathy, students can establish meaningful connections with their colleagues and superiors. Additionally, students should hone their verbal and written communication skills to ensure clarity and avoid misunderstandings.

Collaboration is another key aspect of building effective relationships. Students should be proactive in seeking opportunities to work with others, fostering a sense of teamwork and cooperation. By actively participating in group projects and demonstrating a willingness to contribute, students can showcase their commitment to the success of the team.

Moreover, it is important for students to be open to feedback and constructive criticism. By viewing feedback as an opportunity for growth and improvement, students can demonstrate their willingness to learn and adapt. This not only helps in building stronger relationships but also enhances personal and professional development.

Lastly, students should seek out mentorship opportunities. Establishing relationships with experienced professionals can provide valuable guidance and support. Mentors can offer insights into the industry, share their own experiences, and provide valuable advice for career advancement.

In conclusion, building effective relationships with colleagues and superiors is a crucial aspect of achieving success and paving the way for a successful career. By focusing on trust, communication, collaboration, feedback, and mentorship, students can develop the necessary skills and strategies to foster positive relationships in the workplace. These relationships not only contribute to personal growth but also open doors to exciting opportunities for professional advancement.

Demonstrating Professionalism and Work Ethic

In today's competitive world, success is not just about achieving your goals; it's about transforming your life. The path to success is paved with dedication, perseverance, and a strong work ethic. In this subchapter, we will explore the importance of professionalism and work ethic in achieving your career aspirations and how they can change your life for the better.

Professionalism is the key to gaining respect and credibility in any field. It encompasses various qualities, including integrity, reliability, and a commitment to excellence. When you demonstrate professionalism, you are not only showcasing your skills but also your ability to handle yourself in a responsible and ethical manner. Employers value professionalism because it reflects your dedication to your work and your commitment to the organization's success.

One of the fundamental aspects of professionalism is maintaining a strong work ethic. Your work ethic is a reflection of your values and how you approach your tasks. It involves being punctual, taking initiative, and going above and beyond what is expected of you. A strong work ethic sets you apart from others and shows that you are willing to put in the effort required to succeed.

Developing professionalism and a strong work ethic starts from within. It requires self-discipline, setting high standards for yourself, and continuously seeking self-improvement. It's about taking ownership of your actions, learning from your mistakes, and striving for excellence in everything you do.

By demonstrating professionalism and a strong work ethic, you open doors to countless opportunities. Employers are more likely to notice and appreciate your efforts, leading to career advancements and financial rewards. Additionally, you gain the trust and respect of your colleagues, creating a positive work environment and fostering meaningful relationships.

Success changes your life in profound ways. It brings financial stability, personal fulfillment, and a sense of accomplishment. However, it is important to remember that success is not an overnight phenomenon. It requires hard work, dedication, and consistently demonstrating professionalism and a strong work ethic.

In conclusion, professionalism and work ethic are not just buzzwords; they are the foundation for achieving career success and transforming your life. By embodying these qualities, you position yourself as a trailblazer, paving the way for a successful future. So, let your actions speak louder than words, showcase your professionalism, and let your strong work ethic guide you towards the remarkable achievements that await you.

Chapter 9: Continuing Education and Professional Development

The Importance of Lifelong Learning in Career Success

In today's rapidly changing world, the concept of a traditional career path is becoming a thing of the past. Gone are the days when one could rely solely on their initial education and skills to sustain a successful career for a lifetime. In this subchapter, we will delve into the significance of lifelong learning and how it plays a pivotal role in achieving career success.

Lifelong learning refers to the continuous process of acquiring knowledge, skills, and expertise throughout one's life. It recognizes the fact that learning should not be limited to formal education but should be a lifelong pursuit. As students, understanding the importance of lifelong learning is crucial, as it can greatly impact our future career prospects.

One of the key reasons why lifelong learning is vital for career success is the ever-evolving nature of industries and technologies. As new advancements emerge, the demand for specific skills and expertise changes. By actively engaging in lifelong learning, students can stay up-to-date with the latest trends and developments in their field of interest. This ensures that they remain relevant and competitive in the job market, enhancing their chances of career success.

Another reason why lifelong learning is essential is its ability to foster personal growth and professional development. Through continuous learning, individuals can expand their knowledge base, enhance their critical thinking abilities, and develop new skills. This not only opens new doors of opportunities but also enables individuals to adapt and thrive in different work environments.

Moreover, lifelong learning contributes to building a strong professional network. By attending workshops, seminars, and industry conferences, students can connect with like-minded individuals and professionals in their field. These connections can provide valuable insights, mentorship, and potential job opportunities, further boosting their chances of success.

Furthermore, lifelong learning promotes innovation and creativity. As individuals gain exposure to different perspectives and ideas, they become better equipped to come up with innovative solutions to problems. This skill is highly sought after by employers, as it allows them to stay ahead of the competition and drive growth within their organizations.

In conclusion, lifelong learning is crucial for achieving career success in today's dynamic world. By embracing continuous learning, students can keep pace with industry changes, develop new skills, foster personal growth, build valuable connections, and drive innovation. So, let us adopt a mindset of lifelong learning and pave the way for our own success in the ever-changing landscape of the professional world. Remember, success changes your life, and lifelong learning is the key to unlocking its true potential.

Pursuing Further Education and Certifications

In today's rapidly evolving world, the pursuit of further education and certifications has become more important than ever. As students, you are the trailblazers in the making, paving the way for your own career success. One of the key pillars of success is continuous learning and expanding your skillset through further education and certifications.

Success Changes Your Life

Success has the power to transform your life in countless ways. It opens doors to new opportunities, enhances your professional growth, and improves your overall well-being. Pursuing further education and certifications plays a crucial role in achieving this success and reaping its benefits.

Firstly, further education equips you with knowledge and expertise that goes beyond what you learn in the classroom. It allows you to dive deeper into your chosen field, exploring advanced concepts and gaining a competitive edge. Whether you are pursuing a bachelor's degree, master's degree, or even a PhD, the additional knowledge you acquire through higher education will set you apart from others and open doors to career advancement.

Moreover, certifications are a powerful tool in demonstrating your expertise and dedication within a specific area of study or industry. These credentials validate your skills and knowledge to potential employers, making you a more desirable candidate for job opportunities. Certifications such as project management, digital marketing, or coding are highly sought after and can significantly boost your employability.

Furthermore, pursuing further education and certifications provides you with valuable networking opportunities. Interacting with like-minded individuals, professors, and industry professionals can expand your professional network, leading to mentorship, job referrals, and collaborations. These connections can be instrumental in accelerating your career growth and opening doors to new possibilities.

Additionally, continued learning and professional development through further education and certifications enable you to stay up-to-date with the latest industry trends and advancements. In a world where technology and knowledge are constantly evolving, it is crucial to stay ahead of the curve. By investing in your education, you ensure that you remain relevant and adaptable in an ever-changing job market.

In conclusion, pursuing further education and certifications is a vital step towards achieving success and transforming your life. It provides you with the necessary skills, knowledge, and networking opportunities to excel in your chosen field. Embrace the opportunities for growth, enhance your expertise, and unlock the doors to a brighter future. Remember, as trailblazers in the making, your dedication to continuous learning will pave the way for your own career success.

Staying Updated with Industry Trends and Best Practices

In today's fast-paced and ever-evolving world, staying updated with industry trends and best practices is crucial for student career success. As students, you are the trailblazers in the making, and by keeping yourself informed about the latest developments in your chosen industry, you can pave the way for a successful and fulfilling career.

Why is it important to stay updated with industry trends and best practices? The answer lies in the transformative power of success. Success changes your life in countless ways, opening doors to new opportunities, expanding your network, and enhancing your professional reputation. By staying ahead of the curve, you position yourself as a knowledgeable and valuable asset to any organization.

So, how can you stay updated? Here are a few strategies to consider:

1. Research and Read: Make it a habit to regularly read industry publications, journals, and online resources. Stay informed about the latest trends, technological advancements, and best practices relevant to your field. This will not only broaden your knowledge but also help you anticipate future changes and adapt accordingly.

2. Attend Industry Events: Take advantage of conferences, workshops, and webinars organized by industry associations. These events provide valuable opportunities to learn from experts, network with professionals, and gain insights into emerging trends. Participating actively in such events can help you build a strong professional network and stay at the forefront of your industry.

3. Engage in Continuous Learning: Embrace a mindset of lifelong learning. Enroll in online courses, webinars, or workshops to enhance your skills and stay updated with the latest industry practices. Many platforms offer free or affordable courses that cater to specific niches. By investing in your education, you not only improve your employability but also demonstrate your commitment to professional growth.

4. Network and Collaborate: Connect with professionals in your field through social media platforms like LinkedIn. Engage in discussions, join industry-related groups, and seek mentorship opportunities. Networking allows you to learn from experienced professionals, gain insights into industry trends, and potentially open doors to job opportunities.

Remember, success is not a destination; it is a journey that requires continuous learning and adaptation. By staying updated with industry trends and best practices, you position yourself as a trailblazer in your field, ready to seize new opportunities and make a lasting impact. So, embrace the power of knowledge, keep learning, and pave the way for your own career success.

Chapter 10: Overcoming Challenges and Obstacles

Dealing with Rejections and Setbacks

In the journey towards success, it is inevitable to face rejections and setbacks. These experiences can be disheartening and demotivating, but they should not define your path. Instead, they should serve as valuable lessons and stepping stones towards achieving your goals. In this subchapter, we will explore effective ways to deal with rejections and setbacks and how they can ultimately lead to your success.

One of the first things to remember when faced with a rejection or setback is to not take it personally. Understand that failure is a part of life, and it happens to everyone, including the most successful individuals. Instead of dwelling on the disappointment, use this opportunity to reflect on the experience, evaluate what went wrong, and identify areas for improvement. By taking a proactive approach, you can turn setbacks into opportunities for growth.

Maintaining a positive mindset is crucial during challenging times. Surround yourself with supportive friends, mentors, or family members who can provide encouragement and guidance. Seek inspiration from successful individuals who have overcome adversity and learn from their stories. Remember, success changes lives, and setbacks are just temporary obstacles on the path to achieving your dreams.

Another important aspect of dealing with rejections and setbacks is resilience. Embrace a resilient mindset that allows you to bounce back stronger from any setback. Understand that setbacks are not failures but rather opportunities to reassess your goals, refine your strategies, and come back even more determined. Develop a never-give-up attitude and persevere through the toughest of times.

Moreover, it is crucial to learn from your mistakes and failures. Take the time to analyze what went wrong and how you can avoid similar pitfalls in the future. Use setbacks as valuable learning experiences that shape your character and strengthen your abilities. Successful individuals often credit their failures as the driving force behind their ultimate triumphs.

Lastly, embrace the power of perseverance. Success rarely comes overnight, and setbacks are a natural part of the journey. Stay committed to your goals and keep pushing forward, even when faced with adversity. Remember that success changes lives, and setbacks are just temporary detours on the road to achievement.

In conclusion, dealing with rejections and setbacks is an integral part of the path to success. By not taking setbacks personally, maintaining a positive mindset, embracing resilience, learning from mistakes, and persevering through challenges, you can transform setbacks into stepping stones towards your dreams. Remember, success changes lives, and with the right mindset and determination, you can overcome any obstacle that comes your way.

Managing Work-Life Balance and Burnout

In today's fast-paced and highly competitive world, it is essential for students to understand the importance of managing work-life balance and avoiding burnout. The demands of academic life, extracurricular activities, and personal commitments can easily overwhelm students, leading to decreased productivity, increased stress levels, and ultimately, burnout. However, by adopting effective strategies and making conscious choices, students can maintain a healthy work-life balance and pave the way for long-term success.

First and foremost, it is crucial for students to recognize the signs of burnout. These may include chronic fatigue, decreased motivation, feelings of cynicism, and a decline in academic performance. Being aware of these signs is the first step towards managing and preventing burnout. It is important to prioritize self-care and establish boundaries to avoid overexertion. This means setting realistic goals, learning to say no when necessary, and carving out time for relaxation and leisure activities.

Creating a schedule and sticking to it is another crucial aspect of managing work-life balance. By organizing your time effectively, you can allocate dedicated periods for studying, extracurricular activities, and personal interests. Additionally, incorporating breaks into your schedule is essential for rejuvenation and preventing burnout. It is during these breaks that you can engage in activities that bring you joy and relaxation, such as exercising, spending time with loved ones, or pursuing hobbies.

Furthermore, seeking support from friends, family, and mentors can greatly contribute to managing work-life balance and combating burnout. Surrounding yourself with a strong support network can provide emotional support, guidance, and valuable insights. Sharing your concerns and seeking advice can help you gain perspective and make informed decisions about your priorities and commitments.

Lastly, it is crucial to maintain a positive mindset and cultivate a healthy perspective towards success. Remember that success is not solely defined by your academic achievements or career advancements. It is equally important to prioritize your mental and physical well-being, relationships, and personal interests. By adopting a holistic approach to success, you can ensure that you are not sacrificing your overall happiness and fulfillment in the pursuit of professional accomplishments.

In conclusion, managing work-life balance and avoiding burnout is essential for long-term success. By recognizing the signs of burnout, creating a schedule, seeking support, and maintaining a healthy perspective towards success, students can pave the way for a fulfilling and prosperous future. Remember, success should not come at the expense of your well-being – prioritize self-care, set boundaries, and make conscious choices to achieve a harmonious work-life balance.

Building Resilience and Adaptability in the Face of Challenges

In the journey towards success, every student will inevitably face numerous challenges and obstacles along the way. It is these very challenges that shape and mold us, preparing us for the realities of the real world. To truly succeed in life and carve your own path, it is crucial to develop resilience and adaptability in the face of these challenges.

Resilience is the ability to bounce back from setbacks, to persevere in the face of adversity, and to maintain a positive mindset despite obstacles. It is the key to overcoming failures and turning them into stepping stones towards success. Resilient individuals understand that setbacks are not the end but rather an opportunity for growth and self-improvement. By cultivating resilience, students can learn to view challenges as opportunities for self-discovery and personal development.

Adaptability, on the other hand, is the ability to adjust and thrive in ever-changing environments. In today's fast-paced world, where success is often determined by one's ability to adapt to new technologies, industries, and trends, adaptability has become a vital skill. Students must be willing to embrace change, step out of their comfort zones, and continuously learn and grow. By being adaptable, students can stay ahead of the curve, seize opportunities, and navigate through various career paths with confidence.

So, how can students build resilience and adaptability?

First and foremost, it is crucial to develop a growth mindset. Embrace challenges as opportunities for learning and growth, rather than as roadblocks. Understand that failures are not a reflection of your abilities but rather stepping stones towards success.

Secondly, surround yourself with a support system. Seek out mentors, teachers, and peers who can provide guidance, support, and encouragement during difficult times. Having a strong support system can help you stay motivated and resilient even in the face of challenges.

Additionally, practice self-care. Taking care of your physical and mental well-being is essential for building resilience and adaptability. Engage in activities that bring you joy and help you recharge. Prioritize sleep, exercise regularly, and maintain a balanced lifestyle.

Lastly, never stop learning. Embrace opportunities to expand your knowledge and skills, whether through formal education, internships, or self-study. Stay curious and open-minded, always seeking new ways to improve and grow.

Remember, success changes lives, but it is the ability to adapt and bounce back from challenges that truly paves the way for a successful and fulfilling career. By building resilience and adaptability, students can overcome obstacles, seize opportunities, and become the trailblazers of their own success.

Chapter 11: Celebrating Career Milestones

Recognizing and Appreciating Your Achievements

In the journey toward success, it is crucial to take a moment to recognize and appreciate your achievements. Success is not just about reaching a specific goal; it is about the growth, learning, and personal development that occur along the way. This subchapter aims to shed light on the importance of acknowledging and celebrating your accomplishments, as well as the positive impact they can have on your life.

Achievements come in various forms, and it is essential to recognize both big and small victories. Whether it is acing an exam, completing a challenging project, or even stepping out of your comfort zone, each accomplishment contributes to your personal and professional growth. By acknowledging these achievements, you reinforce your confidence and motivation, fueling your drive to continue pushing forward.

Celebrating your successes not only boosts your self-esteem but also serves as a reminder of your capabilities. It allows you to reflect on the hard work and dedication invested in reaching your goals. Recognizing how far you have come can be a powerful tool in overcoming future obstacles, reminding yourself that you have what it takes to overcome challenges and achieve even greater feats.

Appreciating your achievements also involves acknowledging the support and guidance you receive along the way. Success is rarely a solitary endeavor. It often involves a network of mentors, friends, and family who provide encouragement and guidance. Take a moment to express gratitude towards those who have helped you in your journey. Not only will this strengthen your relationships, but it will also reinforce the idea that success is a collective effort.

Additionally, recognizing and appreciating your achievements creates a positive mindset and fosters a sense of fulfillment. It allows you to cultivate a habit of positivity and gratitude, which can significantly impact your overall well-being. By acknowledging your accomplishments, you shift your focus from what you haven't achieved to what you have, creating a sense of contentment and motivation to continue striving for more.

In conclusion, recognizing and appreciating your achievements is an essential aspect of success. By acknowledging both big and small victories, expressing gratitude, and cultivating a positive mindset, you not only reinforce your confidence but also foster personal growth and well-being. Remember, success is not just about the end goal but the journey itself. So, take a moment to celebrate your achievements, for they have the power to change your life in ways you may have never imagined.

Setting New Goals and Ambitions

Success Changes Your Life

As students, we often find ourselves in a continuous cycle of setting goals and striving to achieve them. These goals may vary from academic achievements to personal growth and career aspirations. However, it is crucial to understand that success is not just a destination; it is a transformative journey that can change our lives in profound ways.

When we set new goals and ambitions, we open up a world of possibilities for ourselves. It gives us a sense of purpose and direction, fueling our motivation to work harder and smarter. Setting goals allows us to define what success means to us personally, instead of conforming to society's expectations. It enables us to take control of our lives and shape our own future.

One of the key reasons why setting new goals and ambitions is essential is that it helps us grow and evolve as individuals. As we strive to achieve our goals, we push ourselves out of our comfort zones and develop new skills and abilities. This personal growth not only enhances our chances of success but also transforms us into more confident and resilient individuals.

Moreover, setting ambitious goals allows us to tap into our full potential. It forces us to dream big and think beyond our current limitations. By challenging ourselves to achieve what may seem impossible, we discover the untapped capabilities within us. As we accomplish these goals, we realize that we are capable of far more than we ever imagined.

However, it is important to strike a balance between setting ambitious goals and being realistic. While it is crucial to dream big, it is equally important to break down these goals into smaller, achievable steps. By doing so, we avoid becoming overwhelmed and increase our chances of success. Setting achievable goals helps us maintain momentum and stay motivated throughout the journey.

In conclusion, setting new goals and ambitions is an integral part of our journey towards success. It empowers us to take charge of our lives, fosters personal growth, and allows us to tap into our full potential. As students, it is vital to embrace the transformative power of setting goals and aspirations, for success truly has the power to change our lives. So, dream big, set your goals, and embark on a journey of self-discovery and achievement.

Inspiring Others on Their Career Journeys

In our quest for success, it is essential to remember that the path to achievement is not one we tread alone. Along our career journeys, we encounter countless individuals who have paved the way for us, offering guidance, support, and inspiration. However, equally important is our role in inspiring others as they embark on their own career paths. By sharing our experiences, knowledge, and lessons learned, we have the power to positively impact the lives of those around us.

As students, we often underestimate the influence we can have on others. We may think that our limited experiences or young age restrict our ability to inspire. But let me assure you, success has no age limit. Each of us possesses unique talents, perspectives, and stories that can motivate and empower others.

One of the most crucial aspects of inspiring others is leading by example. As we set out on our own career journeys, it is vital to demonstrate resilience, determination, and a growth mindset. By embracing challenges, overcoming obstacles, and continuing to learn and improve, we become beacons of inspiration for those around us. Our success becomes tangible evidence that dreams can be achieved with hard work and perseverance.

Another way to inspire others is through mentorship and support. Whether it is sharing advice, connecting them with valuable resources, or simply lending a listening ear, we can make a significant impact on someone's career trajectory. Remember that even small acts of kindness and encouragement can go a long way in boosting someone's confidence and motivation.

Furthermore, we should actively seek opportunities to share our knowledge and experiences. Whether through speaking engagements, writing articles, or participating in career panels, we can inspire a broader audience by offering valuable insights and lessons learned. By sharing both our successes and failures, we provide a realistic and relatable perspective that can resonate with others facing similar challenges.

Lastly, never underestimate the power of networking and collaboration. By building strong connections with like-minded individuals, we can create a supportive community that fosters growth and inspiration. Engaging with professionals in our desired fields allows us to learn from their experiences and gain valuable insights, which we can then share with others.

In conclusion, as students striving for success, we have the ability and responsibility to inspire others on their career journeys. By leading by example, offering mentorship and support, sharing our knowledge and experiences, and fostering collaboration, we have the power to positively impact those around us. Remember, success changes your life, but inspiring others can change theirs. Embrace this opportunity to inspire and uplift others, and together, we can pave the way for student career success.

Chapter 12: Trailblazers in Action: Inspiring Student Success Stories

Sharing Stories of Successful Students and Their Career Paths

Success Changes Your Life

Introduction

In this subchapter, we will explore the inspiring stories of successful students who have paved their way to career success. These individuals have overcome obstacles, pursued their passions, and achieved remarkable accomplishments. Their stories serve as a testament to the fact that success can indeed change your life, opening doors to endless opportunities and personal growth.

The Power of Inspiration

Hearing the stories of successful individuals can ignite a spark within us, motivating and empowering us to chase our dreams. By showcasing the journey of these trailblazers, we hope to inspire you, the students, to believe in your potential and understand that success is within your reach.

Overcoming Adversity

Many successful students faced challenges and setbacks along their career paths. Take, for example, Sarah, who struggled academically due to a learning disability. Despite the hurdles, she persevered, sought support, and eventually graduated at the top of her class. Today, Sarah is a successful psychologist, helping others overcome their own obstacles.

Pursuing Passions

Passion is a driving force behind success. Meet Alex, a student who followed his love for technology and innovation. Starting as a mere hobbyist, Alex developed his skills and founded a tech startup that has revolutionized the industry. His story teaches us that pursuing our passions can lead to extraordinary achievements.

Creating Opportunities

Success often comes from seizing opportunities. Lisa, a student from a low-income background, had limited access to resources. However, she never allowed her circumstances to define her. Through determination and hard work, she earned scholarships, internships, and built a strong network. Today, Lisa is a prominent lawyer, advocating for equal access to education for students from disadvantaged backgrounds.

Embracing Failure

Failure is an integral part of the journey to success. John, a student who faced multiple rejections in his quest for internships, refused to let setbacks define him. Instead, he learned from each experience, improved his skills, and eventually secured an internship at a prestigious company. Today, John is a successful entrepreneur, using his failures as stepping stones towards achieving his dreams.

Conclusion

The stories of these successful students demonstrate that success truly has the power to change lives. By embracing their journeys, we can learn invaluable lessons about perseverance, passion, seizing opportunities, and learning from failure. We hope that these stories inspire and motivate you, the students, to believe in your own potential and embark on your own path towards success. Remember, success is not defined by luck or talent alone, but by the choices you make and the determination you possess. Chase your dreams, overcome obstacles, and pave your own way towards a successful and fulfilling career.

Lessons Learned from Trailblazers in Various Fields

Title: Lessons Learned from Trailblazers in Various Fields

Introduction:
In the journey towards success, there are individuals who have paved the way for others by accomplishing remarkable feats in their respective fields. These trailblazers have not only achieved great success but have also transformed their lives in the process. In this subchapter, we will delve into the valuable lessons learned from these exceptional individuals, who have become beacons of inspiration for students aiming to succeed in their own careers.

1.   Embrace   Failure   as   a   Stepping   Stone:
One common trait among trailblazers is their ability to persevere in the face of failure. They understand that setbacks are not roadblocks but rather stepping stones towards success. By embracing failures and learning from them, they have been able to develop resilience, adaptability, and the courage to take risks. Students should take inspiration from this and learn to embrace failure as an opportunity for growth and self-improvement.

2.   Persistence   and   Hard   Work:
Trailblazers consistently demonstrate extraordinary levels of persistence and hard work. They have a strong work ethic and are willing to put in the effort required to achieve their goals. Students should understand that success is not an overnight phenomenon but a result of continuous dedication and effort. By adopting a similar mindset, they can unlock their full potential and achieve remarkable success in their chosen fields.

3. Pursue Passion and Purpose: Trailblazers have a deep sense of passion for what they do. They have pursued careers aligned with their true interests and values, which has allowed them to stay motivated and overcome challenges. Students should take the time to explore their passions and align their career choices with their purpose. By doing so, they can enjoy their journey towards success and experience a fulfilling and rewarding life.

4. Continuous Learning and Adaptability: The ability to adapt and continuously learn is another crucial lesson from trailblazers. They understand the importance of staying updated with the latest trends and technologies in their fields. Students should cultivate a growth mindset, be open to new experiences, and embrace lifelong learning. This will enable them to stay ahead in a rapidly changing world and seize new opportunities that arise.

Conclusion:
Trailblazers have left a lasting impact on their respective fields, and their journeys hold valuable lessons for students aiming for success. By embracing failure, working hard, pursuing passion, and staying adaptable, students can pave their own paths towards success and transform their lives. The stories and experiences of these trailblazers serve as a guiding light, inspiring students to reach for their dreams and make a difference in the world.

Motivating and Empowering Students to Pursue Their Dreams

Success Changes Your Life

Introduction:

Welcome to the subchapter on motivating and empowering students to pursue their dreams! In this section, we will explore the incredible power that comes with chasing your aspirations and how it can transform your life. Whether you dream of becoming an astronaut, a renowned artist, a successful entrepreneur, or a respected doctor, this chapter aims to inspire and guide you towards achieving your goals.

Unleashing Your Potential:

To embark on the journey towards success, it is crucial to tap into your inherent potential. Every student possesses unique talents, skills, and passions that can be nurtured and developed. Take time to reflect on what truly ignites your spirit and aligns with your values. Embrace your strengths and weaknesses, for they are the building blocks of personal growth. Remember, success is not solely defined by external factors but by the joy and fulfillment you experience on your path.

Setting Clear Goals:

Once you have identified your dreams, it is essential to set clear and tangible goals. Break down your aspirations into smaller, achievable milestones. By creating a roadmap, you can track your progress, stay motivated, and make adjustments as needed. Remember, the journey may not always be smooth, but setbacks and challenges are valuable opportunities for growth and learning. Stay focused, persevere, and never lose sight of the end goal.

Embracing Challenges:

The pursuit of dreams often involves overcoming obstacles and stepping outside your comfort zone. Embrace challenges as stepping stones towards success. Take risks, seek new experiences, and push the boundaries of your capabilities. Remember, failure is not a measure of your worth but a chance to learn and improve. Embrace resilience, adaptability, and a growth mindset as you navigate the ups and downs of your journey.

Seeking Support:

Building a support network is crucial in your pursuit of dreams. Surround yourself with like-minded individuals who believe in your potential and inspire you to reach greater heights. Seek mentors, teachers, and peers who can provide guidance, motivation, and advice. Remember, success is not a solitary journey, and the collective wisdom and support of others can propel you towards greatness.

Conclusion:

In conclusion, pursuing your dreams is a transformative journey that can change your life. By unleashing your potential, setting clear goals, embracing challenges, and seeking support, you can make your dreams a reality. Remember, success is not solely defined by external achievements but by the personal growth and fulfillment you experience along the way. So, dare to dream big, believe in yourself, and take the first step towards a future filled with endless possibilities. Your journey as a trailblazer begins now!

Conclusion: Embracing the Journey to Career Success

Congratulations, dear students, for reaching the final chapter of this book, "Trailblazers in the Making: Paving the Way for Student Career Success." You have embarked on a transformative journey, filled with valuable insights and practical guidance, all aimed at helping you achieve success in your careers. As we conclude this subchapter, it is important to reflect on the significance of embracing the journey to career success and how it has the power to change your life.

Success, in all its forms, has the potential to create a profound impact on your life. It opens doors to opportunities, expands your horizons, and enables personal growth. However, it is crucial to understand that success is not an overnight phenomenon. It is a result of consistent hard work, resilience, and a willingness to learn from both achievements and setbacks.

Embracing the journey to career success requires a mindset shift. It entails acknowledging that success is not solely measured by tangible outcomes but is also found in the lessons learned, the skills developed, and the relationships built along the way. Every experience, positive or negative, contributes to your growth and shapes your future endeavors.

Throughout this book, we have explored various aspects of career success, including self-discovery, setting goals, acquiring skills, networking, and embracing failure. These topics have provided you with a foundation upon which to build your own path to success. Now, it is up to you to take the reins and navigate your journey with determination and perseverance.

Remember, success is not a destination; it is a journey. Embrace every step, every challenge, and every opportunity that comes your way. Embrace the uncertainty and learn to adapt to a rapidly changing world. Embrace the power of resilience and the ability to bounce back stronger from failures. Embrace the courage to take risks and step outside your comfort zone. Embrace the joy of lifelong learning and constantly seeking new knowledge and skills.

As you embrace your journey to career success, never underestimate the impact you can have on the world and the lives of others. Your success can inspire and motivate those around you, paving the way for future generations of trailblazers.

In conclusion, dear students, success changes your life in ways you may not yet fully comprehend. It is a transformative force that has the potential to shape not only your career but also your character and impact on the world. Embrace the journey wholeheartedly, for it is through the challenges and triumphs that you will discover your true potential and leave an indelible mark on the world as the trailblazers in the making.

Milton Keynes UK
Ingram Content Group UK Ltd.
UKHW020924201123
432908UK00021B/3230